Growing Couple Intimacy

Improving Love, Sex, and Relationships

William E. Krill, Jr. L.P.C.

Foreword by Lynda Bevan

Loving Healing Press
Ann Arbor, MI

Growing Couple Intimacy: Improving Love, Sex, and Relationships

ISBN 978-1-61599-387-1 paperback
ISBN 978-1-61599-388-8 eBook

Library of Congress Cataloging-in-Publication Data

Names: Krill, William E. (William Edwin), 1958-
Title: Growing couple intimacy : improving love, sex, and relationships /
    William E. Krill, Jr., L.P.C. ; foreword by Lynda Bevan.
Description: Ann Arbor, MI : Loving Healing Press, 2018. | Includes
    bibliographical references and index.
Identifiers: LCCN 2018020152 (print) | LCCN 2018022422 (ebook) | ISBN
    9781615993895 (Kindle, ePub, pdf) | ISBN 9781615993871 (pbk. : alk. paper)
    | ISBN 9781615993888 (hardcover : alk. paper)
Subjects: LCSH: Couples therapy. | Couples--Psychology. | Intimacy
    (Psychology)
Classification: LCC RC488.5 (ebook) | LCC RC488.5 .K769 2018 (print) | DDC
    616.89/1562--dc23
LC record available at https://lccn.loc.gov/2018020152

Published by
Loving Healing Press
5145 Pontiac Trail
Ann Arbor, MI 48105

www.LHPress.com
info@LHPress.com

tollfree 888-761-6268
FAX: 734-663-6861

Distributed by New Leaf (USA), Ingram (USA/CAN/AU), Bertram's Books (UK/EU)

Contents

For Anne

Acknowledgments

My appreciation has to begin with Dr. David Schnarch; without his book *Passionate Marriage: Keeping Love and Intimacy Alive in Committed Relationships*, this workbook would have never been inspired. Thanks to all of the couples who very truly trusted me enough to *practice* on them in my clinical work, and moved me to begin to create a workbook. Thanks to my publisher, Victor R. Volkman and Loving Healing Press for all of the kindnesses, faith placed in my work, and great editing. Last, but certainly not least, thanks to the woman that I am married with. Anne, without your patience, belief in me, forgiveness (repeatedly) and willingness to give me swift kick when I need it, this book would have never happened.

Foreword

The *Couple Intimacy Workbook* is an excellent tool to help you understand and improve all aspects of your relationship with your partner.

The author takes you on a journey of self-discovery, from your earliest memory to where you are situated now. He explains the reasons/possibilities of how and why you interact with your partner in the way that you do. Your parent's attitude and behavior, both to each other and to you as a child, are deeply embedded in your psyche on all levels. Your early learning/observations at the feet of your parents/role models are how you learned to interact with other people. As you grow into adulthood, you will find that the attitude, behavior and interaction you are repeating in your relationship at the present time does not bring you closer to harmony, peace and understanding of, and with, your partner and the issues you are facing. Clearly this early 'learned behavior' needs to change in order to achieve a better, more enriching partnership.

This little gem of a workbook contains a wealth of knowledge and information and is written in a format that ensures the understanding of the reader. The author identifies the 6 key truths concerning intimacy and succinctly explains their meaning.

After each level of intimacy is explained in full, there follows a task that you are asked to share and complete together in order to enable and assist you in pursuing your journey into a more fulfilling relationship with your partner.

Another interesting aspect of this workbook is how the author identifies the 'negative script' that is indoctrinated in us all. Negative thinking is unhealthy as it promotes negative actions and emotions. There are Automatic Negative Thoughts (ANTs) and Positive Automatic Thoughts (PATs). Accordingly, the job is to swat the ANTS and replace them with the PATS. You need to be diligent and persistent in order to change your negative script into a positive script. Changing our negative script is essential in achieving a well balanced life. Following the author's instructions will greatly assist you in reaching your goal.

This workbook reminds me of a time when I was experiencing problems in my relationship. I couldn't work out and understand why our arguments always ended the same. The same old arguments recurring with no satisfactory end result. No decision or plan to put into action. It was at this point that I hit on the idea that if I wanted things to change, I needed to change the things I was saying to my partner in order to get a different response (I knew nothing about negative scripts at this time). So, the first thing I put into action was not to react to my partner in my usual way. I stopped reacting. I was quiet. I thought carefully before responding. At first, I found it difficult to express how I felt and explain myself to him, but I knew that (a) he wasn't listening, and (b) he would not take on board anything I said. In short, I was wasting my breath. I decided to conserve my energy and make a plan.

In the next part of *The Couples Intimacy Workbook*, the author explains the theory behind the task of making a plan. Many people will find this confusing and, perhaps, unnecessary. However, it is completely logical. It worked for me and the many hundreds of people I have counseled. Forward planning cannot be under-estimated. I want to emphasize that the first part of the plan should identify the process of changing your script by not reacting. You need a period of adjustment and learning as to how to react differently. Making a plan will help to build and maintain a healthy physical and emotional relationship. You plan an engagement, marriage, parenting, holidays, etc. so why not devise a comprehensive plan for your relationship to be intimate, loving, trustworthy, loyal and well balanced? The author makes excellent suggestions for the content of your plan in order to maintain a healthy partnership. This is an essential element of changing your negative script.

In conclusion, I am convinced that *The Couple Intimacy Workbook* is a valuable asset in guiding you into a deeper understanding of yourself and your partner. I encourage you to engage in this fascinating process. I can assure you that you will find this experience invaluable to your future happiness.

Lynda Bevan, author of The 10-Step Empowerment Series,
including *Life Without Jealousy: A Practical Guide*.

Chapter 1: Getting Started – Intimacy 101

Introduction

We live in a hurting world with damaged relationships all around us. The number of couples who stay together once they make their mutual commitment is far smaller than the number that separate, divorce, or simply drift apart. After being in a committed relationship with the woman I am married with for thirty-seven years, and as a clinical counselor for about as long, I have come to the conclusion that issues of intimacy are at the core of couple issues (dare I say, all relationship issues). Intimacy is the central reason why some relationships endure a lifetime, and others seem to last only a brief season. The latter group, if they have children, rarely do the work needed to avoid repeating the same relationship failure again, and essentially doom their own kids to a life of broken relationships. Many people never "get" the central truth about relationship: that it takes hard and persevering work to maintain and grow relationship intimacy, and that intimacy is the tie that binds.

You can only maintain a lifelong relationship through an understanding of the role of intimacy. You can learn the relevant skills needed in counseling, or perhaps a seminar or workbook like this one. Though everyone has the capacity for full, rich intimacy in their relationship, not everyone is motivated to do so. Others lack an understanding of what a healthy relationship is like, because they lack relevant experience. Though some may be able to maintain and enrich their relationship without a spiritual understanding of couple-hood, the deepest possible intimacy between two, I feel, is only attainable with a spiritual sensibility, though that doesn't need to be religion-based.

I unapologetically have offered this workbook from a Christian, liberal perspective. I believe in marriage as something more than a legal agreement, something that is best sourced in a spiritual context with a public declaration, bound by vows and promises, intimately involving God. However, this can be attained without the benefits of the legal agreement and church ceremony. I also firmly believe that folks who find themselves in orientations other than heterosexual have just as much right and potential for a deep, abiding, holy, monogamous marriage and intimacy as do historically traditional couples.

This little workbook will not save your relationship if it is already in serious trouble. That is like using a squirt gun to try to save a burning home. Yet the paradox is, if those couples who are now desperate to save their relationship had done the work in this book, they might have prevented the fire in the first place through essential maintenance work. The vast majority of folks entering committed couple relationships really didn't have the information they needed to be successful, or they were presented the chance to read the owner's manual but opted for the "quick start" instead. Still others may have learned that intimate relationships require maintenance, but have decided that they don't want to do the necessary hard work.

Those couples who find that their relationship is in shambles will need something far more potent than any book: professional counseling. The material in this work-book may in fact be a part of their healing and learning, but there are more fun-damental things they will need to work on if any of these exercises will produce good fruit. Self-help and self-motivated growth is a wonderful and beautiful thing, but most people need some specific support and informed guidance by a skilled counselor to make real progress. Reading about the appendectomy is a good bit different than doing the surgery on yourself.

This workbook came about like most of my workbooks do: clients requested such a structured exercise book to guide therapeutic homework tasks to mend and develop their relationship a bit better and bit faster. Oh, what a delight such clients are!

The workbook is structured to first give a brief introduction to some key truths regarding intimacy, and then to explore some elements that are important to intimacy maintenance and enrichment. For each area, there is a brief reading, then some questions that are intended to be completed individually and then shared with your partner, some ideas on how to do maintenance and enrichment in the key area, a per-sonal exercise (meaning it is not couple focused), and then a couple activity. As you will see in the next section on key truths about intimacy, there is a reason the workbook is structured this way.

Key Truths Concerning Intimacy

Whether or not a couple made their commitment in a religious setting, the vast majority of people live out couple-hood with the ideals of monogamy and yearning for deep unity with their beloved. Even purely secular commitments often hold these concepts of "two becoming one" at the heart of at least the ceremony they choose to commemorate their togetherness. The problem is, these sentiments, vows, and delight-fully poetic words don't come with a how- to instruction book to achieve such intimate unity. Perhaps it is supposed to be achieved through some magical means!

Popular media and magazines touting articles of how to keep love alive will illustrate the shallowness of responses to the deep question of how to hold on to and develop greater couple intimacy. The first key truth is that intimacy maintenance and development is difficult work, which is not as nearly as simplistic as popular culture would have us believe. While love may be considered the primary motivator for intimacy, and they are inextricably entwined, simply having love for someone will not necessarily create a growing intimacy. And low levels of work on intimacy will certainly inhibit the growth and depth of love.

As with any other hard work, there is a need for clear intention. Work doesn't get done without it. How often do we have good intentions to do something, but lack either the will to carry out the plan, or even lack the plan entirely? To be intentional then, for our purposes, is the package of motivation, clarity, having a plan, and then carrying out the plan. So the second key truth is that intimacy maintenance and growth require intention.

The third truth of intimacy comes from the important work of Dr. David Schnarch on couple intimacy, that intimacy *does not have to be mutual or reciprocal to be valid and valuable.* Intimacy can be a unilateral experience, and it is no less real if two people do not experience the same thing at the same time. So often, we feel let down if the other person doesn't validate that they have had as good of a time as we have had, or has not experienced the same intense feelings of intimacy. As if the other's lack of feeling intimate should negate ours. Intimacy development is about what YOU choose to do in the area of growth and development; it is essentially an individual process.

Realizing the fourth truth of intimacy can feel something akin to mourning: that there is a finite limit to the intimacy that is humanly possible. Even if two people are deeply in love, on the same wavelength, and choose to be intimate at the same time, and they share an intense experience of intimacy, they will find that there is, in fact, an outer limit to what can be achieved. They will find that intimacy isn't constant; that healthy relationship requires that intimate times must be alternated with periods of solitude.

The problem, of course, is that we crave an even deeper intimacy than is humanly possible. At this level of human experience, we come face to face with our existential loneliness. Existential loneliness is the deep, constant hunger we have to be filled with *something*. This loneliness is the likely root of all kinds of addictions, from alcohol and drugs to overeating, porn, and patterns of promiscuous sex. It is also the source for many people's sense of stress and anxiety; always trying to avoid any genuine 'down time' or silent spaces where they come face to face with aloneness. Ultimately, this key truth points to human spirituality and our need for God, however you conceive God to be.

A fifth truth is that the clock is always ticking; we always have only limited time to grow and enjoy a life of intimacy. At its deepest point, human intimacy is painful, because some day, we will lose everyone that we love in death. So many couples spend so many years, sometimes even decades, never doing any maintenance, let alone positive growth in their intimate lives together. Indeed, the individual who decides to use this workbook may have the disquieting experience that there is precious little time left with their beloved.

The sixth truth is that intimacy is multifaceted. A useful way to view intimacy is to see its different aspects. A six-fold model might be: intellectual, emotional, physical (non-sexual), sexual, spiritual, and difficult intimacy. Difficult intimacy is when partners need to address an issue that has a high potential for either or both to become emotionally reactive. The entire package of six intimacies needs to be present to be whole, and each intimacy facet needs to be in balance with the other. If any one facet is missing or out of balance, they all begin to be out of balance.

A Word About Men

In most cultures, men may be a few (or more) steps behind women in sensibility and language for intimacy, although some women share this problem. Many men only allow themselves to be intimate under very strict situations, and even then, only for a very brief period of time (usually the milliseconds of orgasm). We men, it seems, equate intimacy with vulnerability and equate vulnerability with weakness. Since no man ever wants to appear weak, we may tend to avoid intimacy, or only allow it under very strict conditions.

I often tell men that it takes great strength to allow ourselves to be vulnerable enough to experience the intensity of deep intimacy with our partner. Only when we can lie in our partner's arms and weep, to totally place ourselves in the hands, heart, and spiritual presence of another, are we then truly a strong and complete male.

Many men will have difficulty with this workbook, and they may resist or disparage the content, or the effort of their partner to increase the intimacy in their relationship. This may be expected, given the aforementioned male experience in most cultures. If you are the partner of such a man (or woman), be patient, do not be discouraged by their lack of enthusiasm or participation, and continue to work for yourself!

How to Use This Workbook

While this is a small workbook, and you certainly could read it over the course of an afternoon, you are encouraged to complete just one section per week. You shouldn't feel driven to complete the workbook quickly, or even one section per week; find your own pace. If your partner wants to work faster or slower than you, don't let this lead to resentment or argument. In fact, if your paces are different, use this as yet another tool to discover the rhythm of your couple intimacy. Working on the exercises should be pleasurable and positive. If you partner rejects participation in the workbook entirely, or loses interest, again, don't be disturbed. You can complete the workbook on your own, and begin to feel better in developing your sense of couple intimacy and its enjoyment. When working through couple activities, simply invite your partner to that activity in isolation, without demanding anything more. If they turn you down for the suggested activity, don't fret, just try again later.

1.1 Intimacy Maintenance and Development is Hard Work

Maintaining and developing couple intimacy is hard work. It takes energy, planning, (sometimes resources), and most of all, it takes a strong desire to do so. Most people admit to being lazy, at least once in a while. Intimacy work is no different; sometimes we are motivated to do it, sometimes not. A fundamental truth is that since couples are two different people, they will have two different levels of drive toward intimacy, and two different levels of motivation to do the work to maintain or develop it.

Because the desire to engage intimately is different for the two of you people, the work of maintenance and development of intimacy is not usually linear, or even at the same pace over the lifetime of a relationship. This reality is one thing that makes intimacy maintenance and development hard work. Another reason for that is that an important aspect of intimacy is that it creates a sense of vulnerability and deep emotion, and for most people, these can be anxiety provoking at least, and outright fearful in the extreme. With deep intimacy comes deep and often sharp, raw emotions and thoughts. It takes a great deal of self-control to override feelings of vulnerability and fear. For many, feelings of vulnerability lead to self-evaluations of being weak, though the two are not the same. In fact, some people know that it takes a very strong person to allow themselves to be vulnerable in the right situations.

Modern life is highly stressful and busy. It takes work to make time for intimacy maintenance and development for couples. Many people are in the habit of consistently placing their own stress reduction on the back burner, even further back on the burner than they put their couple maintenance. Intimacy needs to be intentional.

Finally, the work required to successfully maintain and develop couple intimacy often comes along with the triggering of memories from before we were in the relationship with our partner. Examples are looking for satisfactions from our partner that we missed in our childhood, or the prompting that the work on intimacy does to press us to look at our own character flaws and communication skill deficiencies.

Individual Questions to Answer and Then Share

1. There are two parts to couple intimacy: maintenance and development. Have you personally (not as a couple) worked on maintenance and development through learning activities before this workbook?

2. If not, why not?

3. If so, what are the things you have learned about?

4. What excuses have you used to avoid working on intimacy maintenance and development?

5. At this point, how much desire and motivation do you have to do the work on intimacy?

Intimacy Maintenance Challenge: Identify something you do *routinely* that helps maintain couple intimacy. Think of how you might alter that, even just a bit, to improve the effect.

Intimacy Enrichment Challenge: Identify something you would like to do *more often* to maintain couple intimacy, for example, increasing your rate of giving eye contact to your partner when communicating.

Individual Activity Challenge: Whatever you have identified, do that do routinely; make a point this week to clear your head and really focus and be present to your partner when you do that something.

Couple Activity Challenge: For one week, make a point of holding hands (or some other physically intimate, non-sexual behavior you used to do more of) for at least ten minutes once a day.

1.2 Our History of Intimacy

Our sense of intimacy is formed in childhood. We learn the relevant skills from our family, so our adult competence depends on the poverty or richness of our experiences of intimacy with our parents and siblings. Those things we learn as a child are exceedingly "sticky", meaning that once we get an idea in our head about intimacy as a child, it tends to stay with us, often quite stubbornly, sometimes for the good, sometimes for the bad.

Remembering that not all intimacy is pleasant, as children we may experience all kinds of negative intimacy, ranging from an emotionally ignoring parent to a physically or sexually abusive one. Or, we may experience a kind of intimacy starvation in childhood that makes intimacy as an adult difficult and uncomfortable to approach, let alone learn and practice.

Our first forays into romantic/erotic relationships as teens also have a considerable impact on our ideas about intimacy: what feels safe and what feels unsafe. Most of us come to experience the fact that developing intimacy with someone feels unsafe and anxiety producing, but also can identify that this feeling of unsafe and anxious also has exciting (and therefore erotic) qualities that makes it very attractive. Not the least attraction is the novelty of inexperience in couple relationships, the freshness of exercised eroticism, and mutual discovery of another personality and new erotic pleasures. This is a time in our life that tends to be high risk for being wounded in the area of intimacy. "Once bitten, twice shy," as the saying goes.

If we do not intentionally include relationship education as part of our intimacy history, we may be doomed to continue to repeat the same mistakes over and over again, even long into adulthood. While it may be uncomfortable to learn and put into action new methods of being intimate, it is an important part of gaining greater satisfaction and serenity in couple relationships.

Individual Questions to Answer and Then Share:

1. What do you recall about intimacy from your childhood?
2. When you were a child, who did you feel 'closest' to?
3. Were there any intimacy wounds you sustained while a child? Have you worked through these?
4. If you have not worked through them, how do they impact your current intimate life?

Intimacy Maintenance: Recognize an aspect of intimacy that you craved as a child and did not get enough of, then very intentionally provide that for someone in your life.

Intimacy Enrichment: Dig out old photos of intimate moments with your partner in the past, share the photos together, and reminisce.

Individual Activity: Write down a brief account of an intimacy wound in your past, and note how it may be negatively impacting your current relationship.

Couple Activity: Trade the results of the above exercise, and set aside time to read and discuss each other's accounts.

1.3 Defining Contracts

There are a surprising number of couples who have not spent any time in identifying, defining, or renegotiating the contracts of their relationship. There are three levels of contract in relationship: spoken/clear, subconscious, and unconscious. Essentially, the relationship contract is the understanding of *how the couple will be a couple together*; it outlines the rules of the relationship.

Some of us were raised in a household where there was a traditional male headship, while others had parents who were more egalitarian, or like a captain and first mate, and still others came from a household with no real model of couple-hood because they were raised in a single parent home. Most, but not all, have absorbed the idea of lifetime monogamy, while others embrace serial monogamy (in the cases of breakups and divorces and remarriages), while a few may come out of families that had "open" adult relationships.

Some contracts are spoken at the altar and clear, and out on the table, but many couple contracts are unspoken and subconscious, like "I expect to have an active and enjoyable sex life." Or: "We will live in our own home and not have your relatives live with us." Or: "I want you to be the father/mother I never had." Still other contracts are totally unconscious, like: "Our relationship is about you satisfying my need to dominate someone and have someone worship me." It takes only a little imagination to see how such subconscious and unconscious contracts, not open and clear, or shared by both partners, can lead to serious relationship difficulties.

Over time, contracts in relationship may need to be reviewed and adjusted to fit changing situations and lifestyles. For example, a contract that both partners are employed and have careers may need to be adjusted when twins arrive in the family. A yearly review of the clear, spoken contract, and exploration of sub- and unconscious contracts is ideal, and could be taken up on the recommended yearly couple retreat.

It is a very solid idea that a couple needs to be able to define *how the couple will be a couple together*. It is a solid idea that contracts need to be clearly communicated, understood, and shared. The need for adjustments is a given.

Individual Questions to Answer and Then Share:

1. What are the clear, spoken contracts in your relationship?

2. Do you recognize unconscious contracts?

3. What was the model for you growing up for couple relationships? How were adults in your life couples?

4. Do you routinely reassess and adjust the contract you have?

Intimacy Maintenance: Dig out your wedding pictures or wedding video and watch it together.

Intimacy Enrichment: Write out how you would phrase your vows today if you were to renew your vows…trade versions and blend them.

Individual Activity: Make a list of what you think may be 'subconscious' or unspoken contracts in your relationship.

Couple Activity: Swap the lists above and discuss, remembering to keep a sense of humor!

1.4 Personal Rules of Engagement

Though you both likely made some spoken contract/vow when you committed to each other, each of you may have your own personal set of rules relating to your interactions. For example, some individuals make it a point to never leave the house without saying "I love you", or refuse to go to bed if they are angry at their partner. Some of these rules may be handed down from wise older relatives, others may have been gleaned through self-study or learning through books or seminars. Most personal rules of engagement are positive and valuable tools to keep ourselves faithful to the spoken contracts we have made that represent our couple-hood or marriage.

Here are a few I have discovered and put to good use over the years:

- Never comment on your partner's issues unless *they ask you* for input, criticism, or advice. (You were not asked to volunteer your opinion).

- When you see a very attractive person of the opposite sex, say to yourself: "Wow, he/she is attractive!" and then look away immediately and focus on something else. (Save that energy for your partner).

- If you are unclear about what your partner wants from you, ask for clarification. ("Do you just want me to listen while you vent, do you need help, or do you want a suggestion for a solution?")

- Never let children arbitrarily keep you from a date night. (Only if there is no one available to care for a very sick child.)
- Never hug a member of the opposite sex you are not related to.
- Never have a serious relationship discussion via text or email. (Things get lost in translation).
- Always challenge your negative thoughts about your partner (The negative thoughts are hardly ever right, and lead you to becoming negatively emotional and then behaviorally reactive, and when you are reactive, everything will escalate and get worse.)

Individual Questions to Answer and Then Share:
1. Do you have a set of 'personal rules of engagement?'
2. If so, how did you develop them, where did you get the rules?

Intimacy Maintenance: Find out what your partner's top "rule of engagement" is and determine to learn to use it.

Intimacy Enrichment: Go on a hunt for one "rule of engagement" that strikes your fancy as very valuable and find out what your partner thinks about it.

Individual Activity: Begin to use the rule you discovered until it becomes a habit.

Couple Activity: Share and blend your individuals lists of "personal rules of engagement".

Chapter 2: Breaking Through Your Intimacy Barriers

2.1 Blocks to Intimacy

Many things can block our efforts to improve intimacy as a couple, not the least of which are busy lifestyles, and lack of discipline to 'pay ourselves first' with the time needed to do intimacy maintenance. Issues such as old relationship wounds (think ex's and family of origin), to individual mental health issues (think depression and anxiety), to our own stubborn, sinful nature can serve to stall out intimacy growth.

There needs to be true desire by at least one person in the couple to schedule the time and to create the space needed for intimacy to be exercised. Remembering that intimacy can be very raw and intense, one or both partners may engage in blocking behaviors in order to avoid the intimate space and time created (think: starting a fight). When a pattern like this develops, it is a good indicator that the couple may want to seek out counseling to help them work through the block. Oftentimes, identifying, admitting to, and processing the block can help move couples out of going in circles to positive forward momentum.

Once time has been set aside, there should be nothing short of genuine crisis that can cancel the time together. Even if you are not feeling especially enthusiastic or positive about each other, press yourself to continue with the planned intimate time, though you may decide to change the content of your time together to engage in difficult intimacy rather than emotional or sexual intimacy.

Intimate space needs to be safe for both partners. Intrusions of others or distractions can become stumbling blocks to intended intimacy. Things like setting up safe, pleasant spaces for different kinds of intimacy is desirable. It's hard to have an intense difficult intimacy discussion when you need to pick up the kids from practice in ten minutes, feel emotionally connected when one of you is watching the television during an important topic, or really enjoying sex if there is not a lock on the bedroom door and there are children in the house.

Sometimes you will have set aside time, structured the time well, and yet, once in the intimacy space, you feel awkward. If it has been some time since you have engaged in intimate space with each other, this is a natural and expected experience. Be brave and carry out your planned activities; keep in mind that while you set things up, they may not go exactly (or at all) like you planned. Don't be discouraged if this happens (it happens a good bit), and do not abandon your efforts!

Individual Questions to Answer and Then Share:
1. Are you setting aside time, scheduling intentionally for specific kinds of intimacy?
2. Do you find you or your partner backing away or feeling awkward in your scheduled intimate time together?
3. What practical things could you do to remove blocks to intimacy in your life?

Intimacy Maintenance: "Romance" and intimacy are kissin' cousins: try and make a list of all the things you would like to *remove* to make your life more romantic.

Intimacy Enrichment: Each choose one issue they feel blocks shared intimacy, and discuss it.

Individual Activity: Make clear and concerted effort to change something to unblock intimacy.

Couple activity: Consider doing some work together on your bedroom: give it a makeover in a way that makes the room feel intimacy-safe and erotically inspiring to both of you.

2.2 Words Matter

The language of intimacy is culturally variable. Cultures can range from very large, like entire countries or regions of the world, down to smaller cultures like ethnicity and family groups. Each culture will have its own standard of how it uses language to speak about and express intimacy. It is not uncommon for a visitor to a foreign culture to make errors due to ignorance of traditions or right words or expressions to use. It is also not uncommon for two people who are in love and *think* they know each other to make similar errors. It is important for couples working on intimacy to sort through what common (to the couple) and acceptable (and unacceptable) language will be used to discuss intimate issues.

Language is, of course, much more than just words. Sarcasm is largely a tone and inflection in the voice, and not so much the actual words. Body language is also a major contributor to communication, not the least of which is intimate communication. Anyone who has gotten 'wires crossed' in text communication knows how easily information, real or imagined, can be "read between the lines". So, our words are important, how we choose to use them and how accurately we receive them is important.

A very positive decision is to discipline yourself to think before speaking, to speak slowly, and to take quick moments to affirm that the other person is receiving the words the way they are intended. Equally important is the self-discipline to take a time out from the conversation to check and see if you are understanding things correctly. And still yet, to make repairs to erroneous communication and misunderstandings when you perceive they have occurred.

Individual Questions to Answer and Then Share:

1. Are there particular words in the intimacy arena you find offensive?
2. Do you consider you and your partner to be accurate communicators?
3. Do you pay attention to body language and voice tone?
4. How do you know that you are communicating well?

Intimacy Maintenance: If and when your partner uses a word that you find uncomfortable, say so right away, with an assertive, firm statement.

Intimacy Enrichment: Set aside time to talk for a while about specific words in the area of sexuality that you find acceptable and desirable, and those you find unacceptable and uncomfortable.

Individual Activity: Make a list of words that you feel are very loving and intimate. Make a point of using some of them with your partner during the week.

Couple activity: Trade lists, so you know what words your partner finds loving and intimate.

2.3 Changing the Negative Script

Over time, we can develop a number of negative scripts that run like endless loops in our head. While at one time the content of these loops may have been somewhat accurate and helpful, in many cases they have long stopped working and have become negative to ourselves and our relationships. Einstein said that the definition of insanity is doing the same thing over and over again, expecting different results.

Negative thinking produces negative emotions, and when the emotion reaches a certain critical point (like a pressure cooker), we tend to become very reactive, and reactivity usually results in making situations worse, not better. Essentially, negative means cannot achieve a positive end. Over time, our negative thoughts, emotions, and resulting negative reactive behaviors become an endless 'loop' that we repeat over and over again, compulsively. This eventually produces a sense of beating our head against a wall, and ultimately, produces people who just give up and leave.

Part of this negative looping makes us very self-righteous; we begin to convince ourselves that our *partner* IS the *problem*, and we deny that we have anything to do with it. Get real, of course you are contributing. Your challenge is to first admit that you need to fix YOU. Clear your own negative loops, challenge your own negative thinking, feeling, and doing. Take the plank out of your own eye before you trying to help your partner with the speck of sawdust in theirs.

Needless to say, when a couple are operating out of their own unique negative loops, there are very little feelings of being married, let alone wanting to be intimate in any way. The original, enthusiastic, loving and close team is in grave jeopardy of dying. The need for the negative loops to be interrupted becomes critical, as does the need for the team to become positive once again.

Though it is a tough thing to find motivation to turn around all the negativity, one way to begin this is to "act as if" by engaging in positive team activities, and recognizing forgotten areas of common strengths and goals. It is extremely rare that a couple has lost every last bit of their common goals and cannot come to recognize and be grateful for good things in their partner. They certainly may be stubborn about admitting it, though.

Individual Questions to Answer and Then Share:

1. Can you recognize negative thinking and emotional patterns/loops in your relationship?

2. Can you see how your negative thoughts create negative emotions that cause you to behave in ways that make things worse and not better?

3. Does it feel like you lost your "tea"' a long time ago?

4. In what areas do you feel you have lost it?

Intimacy Maintenance: Begin to make a habit of positively greeting each other after being apart for the day.

Intimacy Enrichment: Make a point of giving a daily affirmation to your partner.

Individual Activity: Determine to be the first one to reach out and positively touch daily.

Couple activity: Make a list of positive ways you have been a good team in your marriage, then swap lists and discuss.

2.4 Intimacy Maintenance and Growth Requires Being Intentional

There is an old saying that goes: "People respect what you inspect". It is human nature to unconsciously (or consciously) let things go. Ideas for good things may come and go in our head, such as something fun to do with our partner, but then the idea drifts away in the clutter of being busy or the resentment we may be feeling in the moment for something our partner did or did not do. (Or we imagined they did or did not do.)

Most of us are intentional and successful in making appointments with our dentist, doctor, or clinical counselor, and almost as successful in keeping the appointments. If we are not intentional about taking care of our own need for rest, relaxation, personal development, and play, this will negatively affect our relationships with our partner, children, and just about everyone we are in contact with. Believe it or not, you cannot have a healthy and growing intimate life if you are not effectively taking care of *yourself* first. Stress is toxic to intimacy.

Being intentional takes checks and balances. Sometimes we need 'accountability' to stick with our intention to do something positive, like diet, stop smoking...or spending time and energy on intimacy maintenance and development. A great way to stay accountable is to have an open, specific alliance with your partner to *commit* to *plan* your work on intimacy together. Remember, though, that, within reason, such an alliance needs to be flexible. If your partner does not hold up the other end of the alliance, resist the temptation to drop the ball on your side of the commitment in frustration or retaliation.

Being intentional also benefits from self-discipline and creativity. When you want to do something, and need to remember to do it, make a literal note of it and stick it to your mirror, or computer, or on the alarm of your phone.

It is guaranteed that there will be times where you have set aside time to plan for or work on intimacy separately or together, and you just won't feel like following through on the commitment. Do it anyway. Remember the *why* you want to maintain and develop your intimate life.

Individual Questions to Answer and Then Share

1. Are you ready to commit to spending time on self-care?

2. Are you ready to commit to doing the intentional planning for couple intimacy maintenance and development?

3. How would you rate your level of desire to accomplish good self-care and greater couple intimacy?

4. How do you currently help yourself to follow through on good intentions to do something (anything)?

5. How do you currently help your partner to follow through on good intentions to do something?

6. What are the things that get in the way of the two previous 15questions?

Intimacy Maintenance Challenge: Look back and see the last time you had a date (without kids). Be intentional about talking with your partner about making a date.

Intimacy Enrichment Challenge: Think about a special, new kind of date activity you'd like to have with your partner, and imagine the details of the date.

Individual Activity: If you keep a personal date book or calendar, write down a small thing to do each day for your partner for one week. This could be anything from a daily hug or an affectionate text, to a chore completion or passionate kiss. Repeat for six weeks, and it is likely to become a habit.

Couple Activity: Set aside time to sit together for about thirty minutes and talk about a big adventure that you would both enjoy doing...add as many details as you can imagine.

2.5 Clarity of Intention

Being clear about what we want is important, and is often difficult to achieve. Much like people who feel hungry, but don't quite know what they want to eat, we can often lack clarity in relationship desires in our life. Some of us may be clearer than others, while yet others may know what they want, but don't want to do the work to get there, or realize that if they get what they want, they *get* what they want, and there are consequences to *that*. (For example, if I become more intimate, my alone time might be compromised.)

Something interesting about intimacy is that once you enter into it at a deeper level, it's not something that you can simply un-do. It's best to be clear on what we want and what getting that will mean for the rest of our lives. Gaining clarity is often a singular and unique process. Sometimes it comes in a flash, other times it is something that must be discerned for a very long time. What do I want? What will it mean if I get it? What implications for the future does getting what I want have? What do I need to learn to be clear about telling what I want?

Remembering that growth in intimacy is largely a personal, unilateral thing (no guarantee that your partner wants to grow when and how you do), it is good to have a structure to help you gain the clarity of intention you are seeking. Time spent in asking yourself questions about the fundamental nature of what you believe about intimacy, committed relationship, and love are good places to start clarifying what it is you want in regards to your intimate life.

You may be intending to simply repair damaged intimacy, maintain the intimacy at its current level, or to increase your understandings, experience, and depth of intimacy. In addition, there may be particular areas or *kinds* of intimacy that you desire to work on and improve. You may want just one, or all of these, but being clear is important, because without that clarity, your efforts may run out of a sense of purpose and energy.

One logical way to keep our intentions in front of us, and make sure they are clear, is to take some time to write out our intimacy maintenance and/or development intentions, and frequently look at them.

Individual Questions to Answer and Then Share

1. Are you clear about what your intentions are regarding intimacy?

2. If you are clear, have you written them down?

3. Do you think you are ready to do the work needed to achieve your intimacy goals?

4. Can you see any undesirable consequences of achieving your intimacy goals?

5. Are you clear on what your convictions are about the nature of love, couple-hood, commitment, and sharing life with a partner?

Intimacy Maintenance Challenge: If you had a ceremony when you committed to each other, what were the words you exchanged? Were they vows? Can you remember them and write them down? Do you still feel that way?

Intimacy Enrichment Challenge: How would you change or add to those words now? Write them down and share them with your partner.

Individual Activity: Think about at least three kinds of intimacy *you* would like more of, then do at least *one* of those things *for your partner* this week.

Couple Activity: Each individually make a detailed list of the areas of intimacy that need maintenance and development, then share your list with your partner to see what overlaps.

2.6 Intimacy Planning

Some people are excellent planners, while others seem to fly by the seat of their pants. While there is nothing wrong with being spontaneous, a good plan is a beautiful and useful thing. In planning to write this workbook, I first created an outline with the broad aspects of intimacy I thought were important, then began the task of narrowing and detailing the aspects, and finally began the actual writing. The reader will note that like most books, there are chapters that organize the effort, and even duplicated structures for each aspect presented.

Planning your intimate life can be much the same as writing a workbook: you might want to sit down and begin to make an outline. The six-fold facets of intimacy are a good place to begin developing a structure to be intentional about. The next step is to begin adding details under each kind of intimacy, and what specific things *you* are going to *do* in relation to those areas. You then can invite your partner to do the same, and then share them with each other to compare notes and come to a unified plan.

A good plan has details about its production needs, meaning what resources will be needed to attain the goal. Though intimacy does not require much or any money, it does need time and sometimes practical planning (stopping and actually buying that bottle of wine or candle, or making sure the bed sheets got changed). Good plans also carry with them due dates for action. Waiting until the afternoon of February 14th is generally not a good idea.

"Best laid plans" as the saying goes; expect that there will be alterations, delays, interruptions, and cancellations to your plans. Life happens. It even seems, sometimes, that life conspires against our efforts to plan our intimate lives. But plan we must, or we will lapse back to that place where we put everything we desire most on the 'back burner.'

Individual Questions to Answer and Then Share

    1. Between the two of you, who has the greater skill and efficiency at planning?

2. Do you make use of that partner's talent for planning, or do you argue about it?

3. If you argue about it, why? Can you find a way to allow input from the less proficient planner without arguing?

4. Is either of you a procrastinator about planning?

5. How much time do you think you would need to set aside to effectively plan your intimate life?

Intimacy Maintenance Challenge: You already know what pet name your partner enjoys you using. Plan to use it at least once daily, and if you already do, double it.

Intimacy Enrichment Challenge: Plan a specific time each day that you will ask your partner this specific question: "Tell me about your (emotions, thoughts, energy, sexual thoughts, and spiritual thoughts) throughout today."

Individual Activity: Time track your everyday, mundane planning chores, like appointments and how to get the kids to their activities for one week. Find a time frame in there when you can spend an uninterrupted hour with your partner for intimacy planning per week.

Couple Activity: Compare notes on the Individual Activity and find and set the time each week you will spend on intimacy planning.

2.7 Carrying Out the Plan

A couple of aspects about carrying out a plan are important, including finding the resolve to be highly determined, and then sticking to the plan. Being determined is different from being intentional. It is the energy and *willpower* placed into executing the plan. While flexibility is a very good thing, don't be so flexible that the entire plan loses focus and falls apart into chaos. There are times when a very good plan cannot be carried out at the time it was intended (kids get the flu, and someone needs to clean up the mess and comfort the child).

Being determined means that the high priority of the plan is a part of it. If intimacy growth and development is a priority, then *do it* and don't let much of anything, ever, get in the way of what is planned. Determination is the *action* of our "will". And our will gets its power from our desire. The will (which is part of the intellect) then goes to work to produce what is desired. The truth is, if you do not have a strong desire to grow your intimacy skills and intimacy experiences, or to be intimate, you won't. If you really don't desire the long weekend in the deep woods cabin with no electronics to interrupt your intimacy there, your partner will pick up on that, guaranteed, and the plan will never materialize into reality.

It helps if you are agreed on the plan and have generated mutual enthusiasm for it; the momentum of enthusiasm can carry a plan when things get tough. Plans get completed more often when couples become positive teams instead of polarized enemies operating from their own trenches looking out over no-man's-land.

Once you have a good, reasonable, and mutually agreeable plan for your overall intimacy growth individually and as a couple, or a plan for a specific event supporting your intimate life, *stick to the plan.* It may seem artificial, and even a bit constricting, but when we alter a plan (especially if done unilaterally), we risk weakening or destroying it (read: resulting intimacy).

Individual Questions to Answer and Then Share:

1. Do your plans to spend time together seem to fall apart?
2. Do you find that your desire, and the success of plans to be intimate, hinges on resentments you are holding toward your partner?
3. What value can you find in following through with an intimacy plan even though you are resentful?
4. Which of you do you think is the more 'full of resolve' when there is a task at hand?
5. Is there a difference in the areas you each have strong resolve in?

Intimacy Maintenance Challenge: Remember something you used to do in the early days of your relationship that delighted your partner, e.g., if you left small notes in hidden places for your love to find. Start doing that again.

Intimacy Enrichment Challenge: Go to the last chapter of this workbook and find something listed there that either appeals to you, or gives you an idea of your own to begin to do for your intimacy practice. Then do it, at least once. If you or your partner like it, do it again.

Individual Activity: Find a resource about how to do good, clear, goal planning, and read up.

Couple Activity: Plan a time together to do something simple, like dance in your living room to 'your song.'

2.8 Intellectual Intimacy

One of the things you probably found originally attractive was your partner's way of thinking: in some ways like you, and just as importantly, in some ways differently. This balance is what makes the other person interesting.

You may recall how you used to be able to spend hours (maybe even all night) discussing ideas, thoughts, hopes, and dreams with each other. Exchanging opinions and learning about each other is an aspect and level of intimacy development common to falling in love. It feels good and exciting to share such intellectual exchanges. But sadly, intellectual intimacy is one of the first casualties of life together. The mundane tasks of life creep in, drudgery of making a living, paying bills, and living by the kid's activity schedule. All this rather inhibits lively intellectual intercourse.

Interesting, intellectual intimacy is a wonderful way to expand a relationship, since we often think we know our partner so well, but the truth is, we are usually just scratching the surface of what we know about this familiar person's thoughts and opinions. Finding where we are the same in our thinking as well as where we are different can bring a sense of closeness that only serves to enhance the other facets of the six-fold intimacy. Good topics can be discovered by returning to things of interest you both have in common, like hobbies, music, sports teams and the like.

I often advise couples I counsel that their married dates should not at all look like their "seeing each other" dates. When on a married date, you are not allowed to talk about kids, money, in-laws, exes, or work. They usually chuckle and state: "Then there is nothing to talk about." Oh, heavens, no, that's not true! Talk about the six intimacies!

Intellectual intimacy becomes an exercise in self-discipline for a couple. At first, it will seem awkward, and of course, you *could* choose to talk about the things mentioned, or you could refresh yourselves by talking about something else.

Individual Questions to Answer and Then Share:

1. Do you recall what ideas and intellectual areas excited you about your partner when you first met?

2. What things do you see as getting in the way of intellectual conversations together?

3. Do you routinely share new intellectual interests and thoughts with your partner? If not, why not?

4. Can you cite areas of intellectual interest you do not share as well as those you share?

5. Do you have a habit of learning about or participating in conversations about things only your partner is interested in?

Intimacy Maintenance Challenge: Find something each day to chat for few moments about that is not about kids, work, or money.

Intimacy Enrichment Challenge: Attend a free or low-cost lecture or seminar that you both might enjoy.

Individual Activity: Read up on a topic that your partner finds fascinating, then fascinate them with your new knowledge!

Couple Activity: Go together to the book store and settle on a book that looks interesting to both of you, then read it and discuss.

2.9 Emotional Intimacy

The ability to share, empathize, and become vulnerable with our partner might describe emotional intimacy. It sometimes takes courage and resolve to share our emotions with our partner (or at least *some types* of emotions). Some emotions we may be more comfortable in sharing than others. Typically, some find expressing anger to be unacceptable or unloving, when in fact, expressing our anger may be a very loving thing to do. For men, expressing the more tender emotions creates a strong sense of vulnerability, and most of us guys equate vulnerability with weakness, and so disallow ourselves from expressing things like fear, tenderness, or uncertainty or grief. At other times, due to resentments, we may try and hide or alter our emotional expression as a means of hurting our partner. There is clearly much work for all of us to do in the area of emotional intimacy.

Having a sense of an emotional bond that is created by emotional intimacy is core to what it is to feeling married; to feeling that what we experience emotionally can be understood, and matters to someone else in the world. When we experience events and accompanying emotions side by side in life, it fosters a sense of bonding that is important to our satisfaction in marriage. Emotions, especially shared ones, function to give *meaning* to our lives.

When emotional intimacy is at a premium in a couple relationship, counselors often hear one (or both) partners express a sense of loneliness, or that their partner 'is just not there' for them. On the other hand, for some couples, a developing danger can be that couples may begin to become 'codependent' and rely emotionally on one or the other far too much to help manage their emotions. They look to each other to 'prop' each other up when things get rough. Mutual emotional support is not 'propping up.' It looks and feels different. Healthy emotional intimacy is a *sharing and supportive* thing; each partner is able to stand independently when that is needed.

Individual Questions to Answer and Then Share:

    6. When do you feel most emotionally close to your partner?

    1. Do you ever feel lonely in your relationship?

2. Are you comfortable with feeling emotionally vulnerable in your partner's presence?

3. Which negative emotions are you most uncomfortable sharing?

4. Which positive emotions are you most uncomfortable sharing?

Intimacy Maintenance Challenge: At the end of your day, ask about your partner's day. Try and identify the emotion contained, and then reflect it back: "Sounds like you had a (frustrating, satisfying, boring, fun) day."

Intimacy Enrichment Challenge: Seek out some favorite poetry or music that seems to create a strong emotion in you and listen for a while, thoughtfully and purposefully. Share it with your partner and explain why it moves you so.

Individual Activity: Try this little experiment: fill a pocket with about twenty pennies. Pick an hour or two out of your day, and every time your emotional mood changes, transfer a penny to the other pocket. See how many times your emotions change during that time frame. You might be surprised.

Couple activity: Set aside some time and find something from your childhood (that you have not told your partner before) that was very emotional and life changing and share it with your partner. Each listener then reflects back the emotions expressed.

Chapter 3: Sex and Intimacy

3.1 Physical (non-sexual) Intimacy

Following the Second World War, there were many orphans left in Europe, and these children were placed in large care giving facilities. It was discovered that despite being fed and kept warm and given needed medicines, the children lost weight. The missing ingredient for them to thrive, as any parent knows, is human touch. Physical touch is imperative to satisfaction in human life. In our busy lives, non-sexual touch may become just another chore, something we are too busy for, or something we withhold out of our resentments.

There is of course, casual, incidental physical intimacy all over the place, from bumping into folks on a crowded subway train to a business handshake to the light skin-to-skin contact while getting your change at the grocery store. But intentional, non-sexual touch is different and far more nurturing *because* of it being *intentional*.

How many times have we heard a person complain that their partner never seems to touch them much unless sex is involved? It is, perhaps, a cultural learning process for males that touch with their partner should or must always result in an orgasm. This is likely because in our culture, boys, as they get older, are touched less and less by their parents, while girls tend to get just as many hugs and affectionate touches as when they were small. Boys tend not to hug each other or hold hands in our culture as girls often do. Due to homophobia, even boys and fathers come to a point where they hug far less than girls and fathers. This translates into the only acceptable place for boys and men to be touched is during sex.

But we men need to grow and mature to a point where we can stop cheating ourselves (and out partners) out of non-sexual touch. We need to get the courage up to tolerate our emotional feelings of vulnerability and start touching not only our partners, but our kids and even friends. Touching others is not only good for our emotional health, but good for our physical health as well.

Individual Questions to Answer and Then Share:
1. What is your favorite non-sexual way to be touched? What do you think is your partner's favorite way to be touched?

2. If you have children of both genders, do you think you touch the girls more than the boys?

3. Are you a good hugger? Do you think that there are different kinds of hugs?

4. What way of touching do you wish your partner would do more of?

5. Can you cuddle with your partner without becoming sexually aroused?

Intimacy Maintenance Challenge: Pick up the pace on non-sexual touch of your partner.

Intimacy Enrichment Challenge: Once you find out what kind of touch your partner wants more of, commit to doing that touch at least once a day for a week.

Individual Activity: Learn how to give a simple relaxation massage (book or video).

Couple activity: Since massages are most pleasant when there is no pressure for reciprocation, set aside (two different) times and give each other a massage. If you are the giver in the first time slot, you become the receiver in the second time slot. Remember that this is not about the massage leading to sex, unless that's the plan in the first place!

3.2 Sexual Intimacy

Most adults think that sexual intimacy is a fairly straightforward and simple thing, and when it works well, it can *appear* to be quite simple, but in reality, it is a very complex and elegant process in healthy relationships. Everyone who has been around the block a few times knows that a person can have sex without any intimacy, or a person can have sex with an intense level of intimacy that can surpass all expectations and enter the realm of the sublime.

Our culture is inundated with sexual images and concepts that often violate our sensibilities of sacredness of sex in our own lives. This constant press wears on us and can acculturate us into buying into a rather shallow and jaded view of sex. We can either come to the conclusion that we are not getting what we deserve, that we are inadequate, or sex is just a chore to be tolerated. Instead of getting the healthy and real facts about human sexuality and our own sexuality, we get taken in by fallacies.

For monogamous couples, sexual intimacy is the only one that should be exclusive to the relationship. One may be intellectually intimate with many people, even incidentally. Or, we can be emotionally intimate with friends and colleagues; physically intimate with our kids and friends, or, if we are in a career such as hair-styling, we may be physically intimate with relative strangers. Still yet, we can be spiritually intimate with others at worship, or even simply one on one with our Higher Power. And in many ways, sexual intimacy can include 'difficult intimacy' at various times in a long term relationship. A secret that few couples come to understand is that it is in sexual intimacy with our partner that we have the potential to experience *all* of the six-fold intimacies *at the same time*.

That sex is physical and emotional is fairly easy to understand, while sexual intimacy having aspects of intellectual, spiritual, and difficult intimacy are harder to grasp. Human sexual intimacy is an incredible, nuanced and sublime communication gift that can truly take a lifetime to master, extract the most from, and experience the very limits of human intimacy in and through. Reaching such mastery requires that the individual is able to engage in self growth as much as engaging in couple growth. It also requires self-discipline to seek out important sexual information from the fields of physiology, emotional health, spirituality, and relationship health.

Individual Questions to Answer and Then Share:

1. Would you like your sexual experiences to be more intimate?

2. Are you able to identify aspects of your sex life that include all six intimacies?

3. When was the last time you have sought out high quality adult sex education to learn something new about sex?

4. Do you feel pressures from the culture giving you messages about your sexuality? What?

5. Do you have any ideas on where to start if you were to decide to learn more about healthy sexuality in relationship?

Intimacy Maintenance Challenge: The next time you invite or are invited to make love, be intentional about doubling the time you usually reserve for this; then use the time to extend your foreplay.

Intimacy Enrichment Challenge: Learn some basic massage techniques and then use them as part of a relaxing and de-stressing gift before you move on to more overtly sexual foreplay.

Individual Activity: Locate a solidly researched, non-pornographic article or book concerning adult sex education, and read it. Take notes, even.

Couple Activity: Set aside time to have an open and honest discussion about a fairly narrow sexual topic, such as which positions you would like to try that are outside of your "usual." Be sure to discuss why a position you would desire is so appealing to you, and likewise, if you reject a position proposed, why you find it unappealing.

3.3 Eroticism

'Eroticism' is the fusion of thinking, emotion, and behavior in our sexuality. It is the *'what'* of what turns us on sexually. What each person finds erotic is quite individualized while at the same time having a universal theme. It is important to note that there is a very wide variety of what even normal human beings find erotic. Each person develops a unique "erotic map" over the course of their lifetime, developing even from a very young age. This is because as human beings, we are gifted with five senses, and these senses make our lives *sensual*. Sight, sound, smells, tastes, and touch all play a role in our understanding and communicating in the world, and we develop preferences and attachments to particular sensory experiences along our way in life (grandma's oatmeal cookies, for one example). Sensuality, or enjoyment of the senses in a sexual way, is erotic.

It seems that eroticism should be just a natural progression and enjoyment of such a wonderful gift as sex, but for many, damage occurs along the way that creates wounds surrounding their eroticism. Things like abuse, or harsh parental or religious prohibitions against enjoying the five senses (or particularly those having to do with sex), can result in adult sex lives that are arid, stale, repressed and constricted, or even consistently painful, both emotionally and physically.

Yet, wounds can be healed (sometimes with the help of a workbook or good counselor), and a person's erotic map can begin to stir and grow again, both in detail and depth. Couples who have been together for decades may think they've explored everything erotic and sexual they are willing to. Even they may find hidden regions of sexual and erotic intimacy, just waiting to be awakened, unwrapped, and enjoyed.

Of course, since our eroticism contains wounds and anxieties, it is often difficult to approach discussing eroticism due to the inherent sensitivity of the topic. When we can create a safe space for ourselves and our partner to reveal our/them-selves, the rewards can be breathtaking.

Individual Questions to Answer and Then Share:
1. Are you aware of your own wounds regarding eroticism?
2. Do you have a sense of when and where those erotic wounds happened?
3. Have you determined what is erotic to you? Do you know your 'erotic map?'
4. If you have unresolved erotic wounds, how might you go about healing them?

Intimacy Maintenance: Choose one of your erotic wounds, and then share them with your partner.

Intimacy Enrichment: Discover a facet of your 'erotic map' that has not been explored, and then share it with your partner. This is usually some erotic or sexual behavior that you have thought about/fantasized about, but have not shared verbally or in behavior with anyone else.

Individual Activity: Choose one of your erotic wounds to focus time, energy, and healing upon.

Couple activity: Determine an area of your erotic maps that overlap, choose an erotic/sexual behavior, create a safe emotional and physical space, and *do it*. Remember not to push your partner to do any behavior that they do not desire to engage in.

*Realize that the above activities will produce anxiety, but follow through despite this.

3.4 Sexual Functioning Issues

There can be many sources of sexual functioning issues, including the development of physical illness, history of sexual abuse, troubled relationships, impaired intimacy maintenance, or a lack of quality sex education. Interestingly, the last three reasons listed are the most common. In recent decades, the tendency to jump to medicines to help sexual issues gives rather false hopes of cures for them. The proof is when we see men take the 'little blue pill,' achieve a great erection, and still really do not want to have sex.

Common issues are: inability or failure during sex to remain physically aroused (maintain erection or lubrication), low sexual desire, physical pain during sex, and inability to achieve orgasm.

Effective treatment of such common issues requires a holistic approach that includes not just medical intervention, or even medical interventions as the primary choice of treatment, but often counseling and education, not to mention a larger view of human sexual potential beyond performance issues like erections and orgasms. Most couples, unfortunately, do not even *come close* to approaching the fullest potential for sexual *satisfaction* in their relationships.

Most sexual functioning problems are a result of relationship issues, and ideally need a couple therapy approach that casts a much wider net than identifying success as the firmness of an erection or the number of orgasms. For a good part of the population, there are unhealed issues of child sexual abuse, relationship problems, or unresolved wounds from coming out as a lesbian, gay, bisexual, or transgendered person that are the root causes for sexual functioning issues. Those seeking help for sexual functioning issues need to be very thorough in checking out the qualifications, therapeutic stance, and cultural awareness level of the counselor they intend to engage.

Individual Questions to Answer and Then Share:

1. Are there sexual functioning issues in your life?

2. Have you seen a medical doctor to explore if medical issues are the cause?

3. Have you sought out a qualified counselor to address other approaches to the functioning issue?

4. What is your current strategy for coping with the sexual functioning issue you may have? Is it working?

Intimacy Maintenance: If you or your partner have a sexual functioning issue, slow down, and work at staying emotionally connected when the issue presents. For example, if one of you seems to lose desire/passion in the midst of foreplay, discuss when the disconnection began, and what you were both thinking and doing at the time. You might then decide to just hold each other, or eye gaze until you reconnect at the emotional level.

Intimacy Enrichment: The next time you have sex, plan to allow for *double* the time you usually set aside, and *slow down* the erotic/sexual process. For example: instead of proceeding linearly from the invitation to sex, rapidly through foreplay, and then on to orgasm, slow things down by 'anointing' your lover's body with fragrant oil, focusing on and enjoying the touch and textures you discover while doing so.

Individual Activity: Determine what you will choose to do if and when a sexual functioning issue presents in your relationship. Determine how you will verbally, emotionally, and behaviorally respond, either in a better way than you have been, or if you have not experienced a sexual functioning issue together, in preparation for the future possibility.

Couple activity: If the sexual functioning issue presents, offer reassurance to your partner by changing focus away from the issue, and engage in some other mutually pleasing activity. For example, if he loses his erection, he might begin to engage her in oral sex, or either of you might begin a backrub for the other.

3.5 Spiritual Intimacy

Spiritual intimacy does not have to be 'religious' or based in dogma, though for most couples, there is likely a history of some religious-denominational experience. For many spiritual traditions, being a couple, being married, and being monogamous has spiritual underpinnings, and marriage is viewed as structure both representing and enriching the spirituality of the participants. At least in the United States, most marriages begin with church ceremonies. Even in coupling without legal or church marriage, the monogamous ideal is often held, which assumes or implies a 'spiritual bond' of some sort.

Spiritual intimacy may include church activity such as worship or service work, and this may be done individually, or as a couple or family. Such activities can serve very well to help build spiritual intimacy for a couple. Couple expressions of spiritual intimacy may be conjoint devotions or prayer, or meditation. Even time spent together in nature can be a shared spiritual experience. Certainly, the exercise of engaging regularly in the other five intimacies can produce couple spiritual intimacy, but this does not mean that spiritual intimacy should be neglected its fair share of attention.

All couples can benefit from the formulation of a 'mission statement' for their couple-hood. Why are you together? (While love is the usual answer, what is being asked here is: what is the mission?) For most couples this is a tough question to answer, and coming up with a mission statement is not an easy task. The mission statement is very valuable, because it can provide a 'beacon,' central point of reference, or core spiritual principle for everything that the couple decides to do in their life together. It can give purpose, measure, and to some degree, safeguard against a drifting away from what the couple has mutually agreed is important.

Here is the author's marriage/family mission statement:

"To create a community of life and love."

Make your mission statement one sentence, and make each word *count*.
Individual Questions to Answer and Then Share:

1. Do you feel your couple relationship is spiritual? How?

2. What areas of spiritual intimacy could be improved upon?

3. Do you have a 'mission statement?'

4. What goes into your mission statement?

Intimacy Maintenance: If you already have a church tradition, keep going! If you do not, consider visiting churches or other spiritual resources to find a comfortable place that will enhance your own and your couple spiritual intimacy.

Intimacy Enrichment: Find a spiritual text to read and discuss together.

Individual Activity: Spend some time praying for /and or meditating on your couple relationship.

Couple activity: Together, craft a mission statement, then post it somewhere in the house that will keep the mission in front of you. Measure all you choose to do by the mission statement.

3.6 Difficult Intimacy

There is a delightfully wise saying that goes: "No sex should ever be safe sex; if sex is safe, you are not doing it right!" The saying, of course, is not about sexually transmitted diseases or pregnancy, but that there needs to be a level of emotional vulnerability and risk to our sex lives that produces growth in overall intimacy in our relationship. Taking emotional risks and being vulnerable is difficult, because it makes us anxious. The same is true about all intimacy, not just sexual intimacy.

While sexual intimacy is usually quite pleasurable, not all intimacy is pleasant. A heated argument is often a very intimate exchange, as is delivering a baby, or shared grief. Some difficult intimacy comes our way uninvited and intrusive, like the intimate news from our doctor of a serious illness. But for our purposes, difficult intimacy is when we have something that is hard to share with someone we love. We may be, in fact, very anxious and worried about just how to word what is in our heart and what is on our mind, but we feel pressed to share the truth, in love. Feelings of intense anxiety arise as we anticipate how the other person will receive what we have to say.

When couples avoid difficult intimacy, they are actually avoiding what can result in great personal and couple growth. The courage and habit of dealing with difficult issues as they arise is how difficult intimacy can temper the metal of couple-hood into a resilient, hardened, and strong bond.

Individual Questions to Answer and Then Share:

1. Most couples have a few things in their relationship that are difficult and ongoing, such as disagreements about finances, for example. What are the points in your relationship that have traditionally been difficult?

2. There is a level of risk and anxiety in speaking your heart and mind. What thoughts are in your head that keep you from speaking?

3. Are you aware of how you avoid the difficult issues? Simply not bring them up? Gloss them over, sweep them under the rug, or joke about them?

4. Do you think there is a way to enter discussion about difficult things so that argument and hurt feelings will not happen?

Intimacy Maintenance: Note the next time you become irritated with your partner and then consciously slow down the process, pay attention to your negative thoughts, take a deep breath, and try calming yourself.

Intimacy Enrichment: Discuss a past issue that has been resolved, and explore the positive results of whatever decisions or compromises that came from the resolution.

Individual Activity: Make a list of the 'difficult' topics that you tend to avoid discussing. Use this list later to methodically address each of the areas of difficult intimacy with your partner. Keep going until your list is cleared.

Couple Activity: Compare lists and choose to address one of the difficult issues.

3.7 *Boom!* Intimacy

I believe that God made humans as a reflection of Himself, and marriage is a spiritual discipline that contains a six-fold intimacy that are the major tools of marriage success and happiness. God intended our sexuality to be most fully and effectively expressed inside a committed relationship that is monogamous, and it is quite (delightfully) possible that marriage can last until death of one of the partners (and likely continues as long as at least one of you is alive).

Because of the gift of monogamy, sex becomes the unique and singular gift of God that can best be expressed and duly satisfied inside of marriage. Though we can go elsewhere for the other five intimacies, only in a freely monogamous marriage can we pursue sexual intimacy. This places the role of sexual intimacy in a key position (pun intended) to effect the greatest aspect of marriage: all six intimacies have the possibility to bind together via sexual intimacy as a *vehicle* for the "boom" intimacy experience of *bliss* and *ecstasy*. This boom experience represents the outer limits of human intimacy potential. Sadly, few people even approach this, because they cannot seem to let go of their stubbornness about resolving the blocks that get in the way.

Understanding couple sexual intimacy as a vehicle for a much higher plane of togetherness may be awkward for some, especially if you have grown up through admonitions that sex is 'dirty' and is far separated from spirituality. Understanding how sex can be the tie that binds all six intimacies together may also be a function of age, and having toughed out the hard work of decades in marriage. It just may be that we need to be old and wise to be able to tolerate the intensity of what the "boom" intimacy experience is. People have expressed that the experience of this "binding together" of the six intimacies in sex is a feeling of timelessness, of expansive unity with each other and the universe, or a glimpse of what heaven will be like. Others describe it as losing their own identity and being joined completely with their partner, or as an experience of holy healing or release from a history of emotional, physical, sexual, and spiritual wounds. One thing is sure: the experience permanently alters the individuals and couples who do the hard work and journey to experience this level of intimacy.

Individual Questions to Answer and Then Share:

1. Have you known couples you have suspected of being at this level of intimacy?

2. Can you recognize this kind of intimacy as frightening or difficult to tolerate?

3. Do you want to grow in this direction?

4. What are you doing to grow in this direction?

Intimacy Maintenance: The next time you make love, focus/search on how each of the intimacies may be present in your present sexual experience.

Intimacy Enrichment: During love making, be brave and talk to your partner about what emotions you are feeling, thoughts you are having, the physical sensations you are enjoying. (Yes, *talk during* sex!)

Individual Activity: Think about a time the two of you were having sex that comes to mind as a fantastic experience. Analyze the aspects that made it so memorable.

Couple activity: Set up a time for you to get away from everyone and everything (see the 'yearly retreat' at the end of the workbook), and come up with a plan to create the conditions where 'boom' intimacy, via sex, *might happen*.

Chapter 4: Intimacy and Your Partner

4.1 Unilateral Intimacy

Human beings are delightfully different from each other; indeed, it is our uniqueness that makes folks interesting to each other. If you have ever been deeply moved by an event, or piece of music, or a film, and discover that the person you are with is not crying like you are, you have discovered that one person can be feeling great and powerful emotions and intimacy while the other is left only marginally affected, or not moved at all.

So often, we expect that because we think and feel one way, those around us should be sharing our exact thoughts and emotions. Some people even get upset if others don't do so. We may not only resent when others do not agree with us on what is important, but interpret their differences as rejection of *ourselves*. If enough people, or a person who is very important to us, experiences things differently from us, we might even begin to question if what we experienced is real.

In his book, *Passionate Marriage*, Dr. David Schnarch illustrates how much most of us rely on the validation of others to be sure of our own experiences and to feel loved. If we have feelings of intimacy in a situation, then we should enjoy them, and it does not matter if the other person or people feel as intimate as we do. If you love the taste of cantaloupe, but I can't stand it, does that take away your enjoyment of it?

The bottom line is that intimacy is unilateral: each experiences their own intensity, quality, quantity, and types of intimacy aside from the other. If two (or more) people experience intimacy at the same time with the same intensity, quality, quantity and type, this is a wonderful gift to be shared and savored. The real trick is learning how to work hard to make opportunities for shared intimacy more often.

Individual Questions to Answer and Then Share

1. Is the idea of unilateral intimacy strange to you?

2. Do you find yourself looking to your partner to validate your experiences?

3. Do you ever feel disappointed or angry when your partner does not feel the way you do? About what?

4. Can you cite an instance where you and your partner experienced a mismatch in how intimate you felt?

Intimacy Maintenance: Take some quiet moments to gaze at your partner and reach inside yourself to feel close to this loved person.

Intimacy Enrichment: Make a point of saying so when feeling especially intimate in your partner's presence. Do not be disturbed if this is not mutual.

Individual Activity: Seek out a place that makes you feel comfortable and recharged, like somewhere in nature. Be 'mindful' and soak in your surroundings, and contemplate feelings of intimacy with nature that you feel.

Couple Activity: Watch a film, listen to a piece of music, or read a book at the same time, then discuss what you each thought was the most moving/intimate part.

4.2 Shared Intimacy

Considering how unique each person is in their experience of intimacy, it is a wonder that intimacy is ever really *shared*. Sometimes shared intimacy happens spontaneously, and there are certainly some situations that it is most likely to happen (the birth of a baby, or gathering for a funeral are just two examples). Shared intimacy is often noted for the deep, satisfying spiritual quality of the experience, as well as its intensity and even life-altering quality. One certainty is that shared intimacy is something that must be *worked at*.

What is meant by 'worked at' is twofold: placing yourself in an attitude of intimacy, and intentionally structuring situations where intimacy can happen. Holding an attitude of intimacy means that we consciously try and clear the resentments from our hearts that may have been building up over time with our partner. There is nothing like resentment to squelch our wanting to be intimate. It may mean that we intentionally engage in 'difficult intimacy' to clear our resentments on a regular basis so that we can hold a more open posture towards the possibility of intimacy with our partner.

Being intentional, and structuring situations where intimacy is focused upon, attended to, and enjoyed together takes very conscious work. Setting aside uninterrupted time to spend together (alone) is a start, and then detailed and elaborated upon. While it may sound strange not to be spontaneous about your intimate life, and spontaneity is in fact fun, busy lives leave little time for it. It is a fact of couple-hood: shared intimacy must be planned for if it is going to happen with any satisfying regularity.

Individual Questions to Answer and Then Share:

1. Can you cite some spontaneous, or naturally occurring instances of shared intimacy in your life with your partner?

2. Does the idea of planning for shared intimacy seem awkward to you?

3. How many times in the history of your relationship have the two of you been truly 'alone' for an extended period of time (not in a restraint or on vacation with family or friends)?

4. Do you find that your resentment list toward your partner dampens your desire to be intimate?

Intimacy Maintenance: Find out what your partner needs more of to feel loved; then do that, often.

Intimacy Enrichment: Choose and agree upon a time to do an intimacy experiment: make love, and afterward be ready to share what parts were most meaningful and intimate for each of you; see if anything overlaps.

Individual Activity: Plan and structure an event that gives you both a chance to share one of the intimacies.

Couple Activity: Share the plan above with your partner and then carry it out.

4.3 Asking for Intimacy

Aside perhaps from directly asking for sexual intimacy (and not everyone does that), most people have no idea of how to appropriately ask for intimacy engagement with their partner. Central to asking for intimacy is knowing which of the intimacies you are looking for, and *time*.

When we pause and take a moment to think about what exactly we want intimately with our partner at any given time, we can be far more specific and clear than usual. Time is important, because intimacy requires a kind of *focus* and *intention* that has a higher quality when proper time is set aside for it.

What blocks us from asking clearly and setting aside intentional time are our emotional reactions and resulting anxiety and resentments. When people are emotionally reactive, they gather a long list of resentments, and begin to think negative things about their partner. When this happens, they tend to either seek intimacy in an indirect, roundabout way, or stop seeking it entirely, and then become even more resentful. A vicious cycle begins between the couple.

It is essential that individuals make a habit of monitoring their own list of resentments and work at resolving them, because if they do not, they will fail to ask for the intimacy they need and desire. Eventually, very elaborate games begin to be played, both consciously and unconsciously, and the scoreboard gets so full that it threatens to topple over. It can get so bad that people feel too awkward or needy, or resentful to even ask for a simple hug to reconnect. The 'cold wars' continue to escalate toward the inevitable nuclear exchange, and there are never many survivors of that.

By slowing down, by knowing what you desire, by making time intentionally, by calming yourself, by releasing your resentments, you can become clear in communicating what you are looking for regarding intimacy with your partner. Oh, and it is important to understand that your partner cannot read you mind, and you will have to likely do this *each and every time you desire an intimate exchange*. Just like we tell someone we love that we love them many more times than once, we have to continue to ask for the intimacy we desire.

It is helpful to make use of the six-fold intimacy model to do the asking. First, figure out what kind of intimacy (or combination of intimacies) you want, then have a plan for what behaviors, time, and resources will be needed to experience the intimacy, and then to determine the right words to use in your asking process.

Individual Questions to Answer and Then Share:

1. How clear do you think you are when you approach your partner for intimacy?

2. Do you think your partner is clear when approaching you for intimacy?

3. What do you think about the idea that 'unclear communication' is more about your feelings in the moment than actual communication skills?

4. What is the hardest part in the process of asking for intimacy?

Intimacy Maintenance: Be conscious of your non-sexual physical touch, and make it a point to daily touch your partner in a way that you know satisfies.

Intimacy Enrichment: Have a bit of fun: find some song lyrics, choose a brief phrase that works for the kind of intimacy you want, and sing the lyrics to playfully invite intimacy. Example: "Feel Like Makin' Love" by Bad Company.

Individual Activity: Work on establishing a kind of formula way of asking for intimacy from your partner. Though it can contain 'code word' be sure it is clear, direct, and brief.

Couple Activity: For each of the six intimacies, explore together different ways that are comfortable/acceptable to both of you to ask for or invite intimacy.

4.4 Choosing To Decline Intimacy

The dance of initiating and accepting an invitation to intimacy is complex and full of meaning and nuance. It's not just agreeing on what the two of you will have for dinner. After all, even in a bistro you get a choice from the menu. If each time you went out to dinner, your partner insisted you eat the very same dish on the menu, you would likely stop enjoying going out to dinner.

Choosing and learning how to decline an invitation to intimacy is a very healthy and important thing to gain. The pressure to always say yes to intimacy is likely to lower the quality of that intimacy. No one likes to feel that they *have* to engage in any of the six intimacies. You have an inalienable *right* to choose not to be intimate in any particular situation (all except, perhaps, if you are a woman and are giving birth!).

Many people get into the bad habit of *pushing* their partner away, or *sabotaging* their partner's invitations to intimacy as a means of declining an invitation. It does not take too much imagination to understand how fast that approach gets old, not to mention how destructive it is in the long run. Others develop an 'ignoring' strategy, acting as if they do not realize their partner is making the invitation, or ignoring the amount of time since they have chosen to engage in intimacy with their partner. This too, takes a terrible toll on the relationship.

A better way to decline an invitation to intimacy is not to push away, not to ignore, not to pick a fight, not to make an excuse, but to simply respond something like, "I recognize your invitation, but just now I am not feeling like I want to be intimate in that specific way. I love you and care about your desire to be intimate, but I don't want that right now."

Individual Questions to Answer and Then Share

1. Do you feel free to decline intimacy with your partner?
2. Which kinds of intimacy are easier or harder to decline?
3. What is the quality of intimacy that is lost for you if you feel pressured to intimacy?
4. Looking at each of the six intimacies, is there a difference in how inviting and declining are done?

Intimacy Maintenance: If you are the one asking for or inviting intimacy, try and remember to tag on an appropriate qualifier from time to time. For example: "I'd like to make love, but I want to be sure you don't feel pressured to say 'yes' right now."

Intimacy Enrichment: If you are the one declining the intimacy, try and remember to offer a small consolation, like a warm hug.

Individual Activity: When you are asked/invited to intimacy, discipline yourself to pause (briefly!) before you say 'yes' or 'no,' and give yourself time to consider the invitation.

Couple Activity: Discuss a communication method that you both can use if, in the middle of intimacy, one of you begins to feel disconnected, wants to take a break, or wants to end the intimate encounter. How can you be clear and kind about communicating these to your partner?

4.5 Handling a Declined Invitation

When we choose to initiate intimacy, we are in a very vulnerable position: the other person can choose to decline, and no one likes to be turned down. Like it or not, each of us can turn into a pouty two year old when we ask for the cookie (or whatever) and are told no.

Indeed, we adults have a variety of reactions when we are declined, from literal pouting to 'shut down,' to resentment, score keeping, anger, and rage. Sadly, some hold the grudge so intently that they simply give up and eventually stop asking, initiating, or inviting intimacy.

Just like when we refuse to give a cookie to a child (usually moments before dinner), it does not mean we do not love them, so too declined intimacy does not mean our partner does not love us or is rejecting *us*. Learning how to gracefully accept a declined invitation is a key attitude and skill to gain for long term intimacy building.

If managed properly, being declined when we invite can be a learning experience: we can examine why we were declined, study the conditions under which we made the invitation, and gain wisdom, or learn ways to 'pitch' differently that are more appealing to our partner. We can use declined invitations to examine our own style of coping with disappointment at being declined, and perhaps discover character flaws in ourselves that we can begin to address in a positive fashion.

It is altogether fair and good to challenge a partner who consistently declines to pay attention to the frequency of declinations. It is reasonable to be disturbed, hurt, or to feel lonely when repeated invitations get turned away. It is then our responsibility to enter the space of difficult intimacy to share our thoughts and feelings with our partner.

Individual Questions to Answer and Then Share:

1. What is your bad-habit-reaction when your efforts to initiate intimacy are declined?

2. What are your negative thoughts when you are declined? Do they have to do with your self-esteem?

3. How would you describe the difference between a declined invitation to say, sex and a rejection of *you*?

Intimacy Maintenance: Check yourself to see if there are times when you have the urge to initiate intimacy (any of the six), but you get right up to the moment and then do not make the invitation. When this happens, press yourself to ask anyway.

Intimacy Enrichment: Remind yourself that it is not necessary for your partner to reciprocate for you to feel intimate. For example, you may notice how sometimes you just watch your partner for a few moments and feel an overwhelming wave of affection, love, or physical attraction. This feeling of intimacy is not made null and void by the other person not knowing what you are doing, declining your hug, or your efforts to start a conversation, or the fact that they may protest your compliment of how good they look.

Individual Activity: Design a positive, comfortable, brief, but clear statement in response to a declined invitation, and begin to use it regularly. For example: "OK, but I want you to know how much I love (talking with you, holding you, sharing with you, making love with you, praying with you)."

Couple Activity: When one of you declines an invitation to intimacy, take a moment and determine a time in the near future to engage in the intimacy that was requested.

4.6 The Role of Power in Intimacy

Like it or not, power is a central fact in couple relationships: who has it, who uses it, how it is used or shared (and abused), and how it changes throughout the history of the relationship. Power pervades relationship, in all aspects and all areas. The nature of the relationship determines the expression of power. Is your relationship modeled on headship, or do you have an egalitarian model of partnership? Whether you're legally married or not may be relevant. Are there others from outside the relationship who interfere? Power issues can serve to enhance or block intimacy expression and growth.

In the time of our grandparents, couples are considered to have had clearly divided powers: women ruled the home, while men ruled everything else (including the female). This is in fact, a vast exaggeration, as our grandparents' generation had as many issues with power and intimacy as we do. As a result of feminism, couple power became more openly balanced, and for the positive. Yet one of the drawbacks of the feminist movement is that people began to believe that power in couple relationships always has to be shared and equal in all areas of the couple's lives. Strict adherence to such a 'politically correct' position has the distinct possibility of stalling, confusing, or repressing most of the six intimacies mentioned, not the least of which is sexual.

For example, what if a couple, living an egalitarian relationship, extends this equal-power- always dynamic into their sex life? What if one partner longs to be swept off their feet with passion, yielding to their partner's assertive and commanding erotic behaviors, but the partner feels anxious about grabbing erotic power and using it that way?

Or, what if one partner consistently defers to the other's position on just about everything because the other partner has a talent for becoming highly emotional in a way that pressures the other to comply?

In still another example, what if neither partner can seem to make a choice without the other partner's full and unequivocal agreement?

Individual Questions to Answer and Then Share:

1. How is power shared or used in your relationship?

2. Are there different areas where one of you has more power than the other? Is it agreeable to both of you?

3. If someone wants more power in one area, or if one partner is abusing power, it can severely dampen the desire to move toward intimacy. Can you think of instances of this in your relationship?

4. What kind of relationship best describes yours: headship, egalitarian, or something else?

Intimacy Maintenance: For about a week, note to each other when a power decision is made, and by whom. For example, who makes the decision to go out to eat? Who decides who will do what chore? Who usually initiates sex?

Intimacy Enrichment: Discuss which of you usually takes the lead in sexual encounters, and then plan a time to have sex. The game is that the person who usually takes the lead must be passive and allow the other one to lead the entire sexual encounter.

Individual Activity: Decide an area of your relationship where you would like to have more power. Jot down a few notes regarding the area, why you want more power in that area, and how having more power in the area might increase your couple intimacy.

Couple Activity: Set aside time to talk about the individual activity. Be sure to monitor yourself and stay calm: the exercise in not meant to turn into an argument!

Chapter 5: Expanding Intimacy

5.1 Human Intimacy is Limited

Almost every human being has a strong drive and desire to become special, to be understood, to be cared for and loved by someone else. Our culture and media give us an ideal image of intimacy that is oversimplified and exaggerated. When our real life experiences of relationships fall short of what we see in the movies, we can become disillusioned, or even depressed. Add to this all the ways we intentionally and unconsciously place barriers to intimacy in our lives, it is a wonder any of us find any intimate satisfaction.

The truth, though, is that the movie fantasies of intimacy are not real. Real intimacy is far harder work, and is far more difficult to live with. The even deeper truth about intimacy is that there is a limit to human intimacy; no human being will ever get as close to us as God does. Even if you are an atheist, you might agree that because you and your partner are different beings, there is a limit to how close you can get.

When we ultimately face this truth at the deepest level (that we are alone), and only God can satisfy our deepest craving for unity, the experience of intimacy can be daunting. Yet, even though human intimacy has limitations, most human beings fail to do the work you are doing right now: learning how to achieve enriched and beautiful depths of intimacy that *are* humanly possible.

Those who take up the challenge to actualize their full potential in the area of human intimacy will find that it is truly an enriching and life-changing endeavor. Even when we find ourselves in unfamiliar and intense territory of intimacy with our partner, we have the potential to be able to learn to calm ourselves enough to enjoy it. Intimacy at this level gives meaning to life.

Individual Questions to Answer and Then Share

1. On a 0 to 99% scale, how would you rate your current level of overall intimacy in your life?

2. Can you identify the things that block your achieving greater intimacy satisfaction in your life?

3. When most people are brutally honest with themselves, one of the blocks to greater intimacy is fear. What do you fear about greater intimacy?

4. Can you 'touch' the place inside you that craves a kind of intimacy that no human can satisfy?

Intimacy Maintenance: Check your schedules or calendars together: are there intentional times set aside and structured for all six intimacies on it? If not, do so!

Intimacy Enrichment: Plan an event around one or two of the six intimacies that has the potential to clearly advance intimacy in your relationship. Be specific, and then carry out the activity!

Individual Activity: Once you have discovered a behavior you can do that helps your partner feel close to you, create a plan and secure the means for increasing the rate at which you provide this.

Couple Activity: Each choose one of the intimacies and write out a brief fantasy representing the pinnacle you imagine that could be reached together, then exchange the stories, and discuss.

5.2 Willingness to Move Outside of Our Comfort Zone

Intimacy is not always light, playful, and enjoyable; it can make us feel uncomfortable (ask any woman who has experienced the intimacy of birthing a baby). Along with intense episodes of intimacy, we may experience a good bit of anxiety, even when the intimacy is passionate and very pleasurable. This is because while intimacy implies a "joining," this joining can feel threatening to our own sense of self-identity. It is the nature of intimacy to lose yourself, to have consciousness diffuse, and this can feel uncomfortable indeed.

To be intimate takes a measure of courage, and to intentionally grow intimacy means having to move outside of your comfort zone to engage in a wider variety of behavioral experiences, even ones that may make you feel a bit anxious. No one should ever engage in a behavior that they truly reject in, but don't automatically discount an activity simply because it initially does not seem to interest you. For example, when you were very young, you may have witnessed a couple kissing with their mouths open, and may have felt simple mystification or even disgust, not seeing the point of such a behavior. Upon the first time you actually kissed that way, you were likely quite anxious, but once you experienced it, came to very much enjoy the behavior.

Successful, shared navigation of anxiety that accompanies a new intimate behavior produces a sense of intimacy and bonding. This is not an uncommon effect of say, soldiers who have gone through battle together. While couple relationships may not be battles (though sometimes may feel like it), the principle is still the same. Growth tends to produce discomfort: we may want the goal, but we do not want to do the uncomfortable work to get there.

It also must be kept in mind that while one partner may be willing to experience some discomfort in regard to intimacy, there is no guarantee that the other partner is willing to do so. This should never dissuade the person who desires to grow, or upset the person who is not ready. Understanding the elegance of couple-hood means understanding that good growth for our partner is good future growth for ourselves. The two of you can either have a negative effect on each other, or a positive one. This is your (individual) choices.

Individual Questions to Answer and Then Share:

1. Think about the beginning of your relationship: what intimacies did you most feel cautious, or uncomfortable with?

2. Which intimacy with your partner required the most courage for you to engage in?

3. How about the two questions above in the present?

4. Is there an intimate activity (not necessarily sexual) that you once felt very anxious about with your partner, and now don't?

Intimacy Maintenance: Most couples like different kinds of music or films. Go out of your way to be willing to experience music or a film that your partner enjoys.

Intimacy Enrichment: Discuss and decide on an intimate activity that you both find relatively anxiety producing, and then make careful, detailed plans of how the activity would be carried out. Examples: If in your judgment your partner would love to care for you and ensure you have a good time while camping, but you have always preferred comfort, then go try camping! Or, if you are not comfortable having sex with the lights on, try lighting a number of candles, for a softer lighting effect.

Individual Activity: You may have a fairly good idea of an intimate behavior that your partner enjoys or wants to try. Determine the time, place, and details of offering to engage in this activity. Have courage: if you try, and find out that you really dislike the behavior, you never need to do it again. If you feel neutral about it, then it can become a loving gift to your partner.

Couple Activity: Do the Intimacy Enrichment activity you planned. Caution: only engage in the activity if you both genuinely desire to try it, and resist any temptation to pressure each other if one of you decides at the last moment to draw back.

5.3 Misinterpreted Desire

Even very skilled in communicators will tell you that communication can easily go awry and become confusing, resulting in hurt feelings. When couples have been together for even a short time, they can become fearful and overcautious about how they share their thoughts, emotions, and desires to each other. As a result, communication gets skewed, and each may begin to jump to conclusions about what the other's real intentions are. The result is often two people resentful toward each other, arguing about something that is not even really true. A classic example is when one partner concludes the only time the other gives a hug is when sex is wanted.

While it may or may not be true that your partner may have sex on their mind when hugging you, you won't really know unless you ask. Even better, when you hug and have sex on your mind, you might just try saying so. Instead of beating around the bush for what kind of intimacy and what intimate activity you want, develop the healthy habit of speaking clearly.

Many couples complain that their problem is communication. What genuinely happens is that the process of clear communication degrades as each partner begins a process of reacting to the other. One of the major effects of this emotional reactivity is that people not only stop speaking clearly, they stop speaking at all. This is a logical, but not workable solution. We grow silent because we get the distinct feeling that there is nothing we can say that won't upset the other person, or what we have to say falls on deaf ears, or, we are so angry that we try and emotionally shut out or hurt our partner. At this point, the communication is exceedingly clear: "I am pissed off at you, and don't want to communicate." The person's intent and desire is clear: to strike back and hurt the other.

Individual Questions to Answer and Then Share:

1. Are you guilty of jumping to conclusions? Can you cite an example where you do that repeatedly in your relationship?

2. What makes you so certain that your jumped-to-conclusion is right? Because you have been right in the past? Even if that's true, does it make logical sense that you will always be right about your jumped-to-conclusion?

3. Do you tend to 'beat around the bush?' Can you cite and example where you do that repeatedly in your relationship?

4. Do you 'beat round the bush' because you fear your partner rejecting your request for intimacy? Do you realize that not being clear and direct can lead them to misunderstanding?

Intimacy Maintenance: Find something simple you can both agree on easily, like, "I need my daily hug!" and then both practice that for a week or so. Better yet, begin to make it a habit!

Intimacy Enrichment: Take *time* when discussing intimate issues, be *gentle* with each other, be *thorough*, asking questions of your partner like, 'What are your thoughts?' and 'How do you feel right now?'

Individual Activity: Make a commitment to yourself to become clearer in how you communicate what you want, and to monitor yourself from jumping to conclusions before you even *listen* to your partner.

Couple activity: Tell each other which intimacy you would like more of.

5.4 Clear Communication Feeds Intimacy

Everyone wants to have clear communication, and every couple cites 'communication' as a problem in their relationship. In fact, people are often communicating quite well and clearly, if we take the time to study and interpret the 'language' they use. Most of us know that communication is more than words. It is also 'body language' and the broad behavior sets we routinely engage in. Yet, many people either do not take the time to develop the skills of interpretation, are too lazy to do so, choose not to, or intentionally give mixed messages to deceive, confuse, and hurt the other person. In yet other cases, an individual may ask for intimacy, but has a hard time dealing with its intensity, and so uses confusing communication. Words give one message, while things like tone of voice, posture, body tension give the opposite.

And so, 'clear communication' begins with *self-honesty:* stop giving false messages! Have the courage to speak what is genuinely in your heart and on your mind. Avoid 'mumbo-jumbo' talk or use of clichés from soap operas, or psychobabble from television psychologists in clever sound-bytes. In essence, become *real*.

Genuine, clear, effective and intimacy-building communication is not difficult to do once you decide for yourself that you are going to stop playing childish games that include score-keeping, revenge, manipulation, trickery, playing dumb, or being so wishy-washy you never state your desires and needs.

Genuine, clear, effective communication waters intimacy like spring rains, and brings beautiful fresh greenery and colorful fragrant flowers of intimacy, making being together a more consistent delight.

Individual Questions to Answer and Then Share:
1. Do you routinely and consciously study and correctly interpret your partner's overall communication?

2. If you are unsure, do you ask, or do you just assume you understand?

3. Can you get in touch with your own manipulation of communication in your intimate life?

4. Are you able to commit yourself to communicating more clearly as an act of personal integrity?

Intimacy Maintenance: Over the course of a week, commit yourself to paying as much attention to your partner's non-verbal communication as to their verbal communication.

Intimacy Enrichment: Set aside time to give each other a really good backrub (no words). Afterward, discuss what you communicated with each other during the experience.

Individual Activity: Make it a point to begin a habit of looking into your partner's eyes when speaking with each other. If eye contact is not returned, ask for it.

Couple Activity: The next time you both start talking about having sex, each should do the following: state what specific sexual behaviors you would like to engage in, what emotions you hope to feel during and after the sexual encounter, and who will take the lead in carrying out the plan.

5.5 Solitude Feeds Intimacy

There is an old saying that absence makes the heart grow fonder. While there are many ways to interpret this, it has truth in that we need 'space' and quiet in our lives to be healthy.

Solitude means *productive* alone time. Just spending time alone is not enough. We need to plan that time intentionally to produce something good. Often, it means we need more than just an hour or two break from our usual life, and set aside a whole day or a few days for the time of solitude.

Taking time for solitude means that we separate ourselves from the everyday, get away from the constant din of busyness that we are used to. It could mean a walk in the park, or meditation near a creek or river, or a long walk on the beach. The time should be used in introspection, taking inventory of our life, and listing all the things we are grateful for.

This solitude feeds intimacy in several ways. First, time away lends perspective on our life and relationships, and allows us to consider why and how we love those around us. Once we appreciate this, we can then convince ourselves of ways we have not been so loving, or ways in which we have been negligent to our partner. Without the away time and space of solitude, we can get a feeling of being smothered by the closeness of intimacy. And so, healthy intimacy requires periods of solitude; it is the balance of intimacy and solitude that enhances each.

Individual Questions to Answer and Then Share:
1. How comfortable are you spending time alone for extended periods (more than a couple of hours)?
2. Do you schedule such times into your life?
3. What do you do (or would you do) if you have time to spend in solitude?
4. Do you feel comfortable encouraging your partner to spend time in solitude?

Intimacy Maintenance: Every day for a week, plan to spend some time before you sleep in reviewing your day and making a list of things you are grateful for (you might even pray).

Intimacy Enrichment: Go someplace quiet together, like a park, the woods, or near water, and sit together, but without speaking. Use the time to meditate about your life together. Hold hands if you wish.

Individual Activity: Begin to schedule an activity that affords you solitude at least monthly; be sure that you schedule enough time for the 'quiet to sink in,' and choose an activity that feeds your spirit, and calms you, or brings you great joy. A good hint is to look at things you used to do before your relationship that you loved doing, but have gone by the wayside in your busy life.

Couple Activity: Be sure to greet your partner warmly after their time in solitude, and ask, but do not press about your loved one's time in a quiet space.

5.6 The Clock is Ticking

Life has a time limit for each of us. "The clock is always ticking" is very true: we only have so much time to enjoy life. Life is busy and stressful and we usually end up chasing after many things that ultimately do not satisfy us. We work hard to pay bills, to collect enough money to retire, and engage in all kinds of necessary activities, but may fail to prioritize what is really important until it is too late.

Creating satisfying intimacy takes time, energy, and work, and sometimes a conscious dedication of monetary resources (or sacrifices) to achieve. What good is all of our expended energy on work and making money and collecting stuff, if we have no satisfying relationships to share it in?

For many people who reach their third and fourth decade with the same partner, we come to see in hindsight the incredible journey we have made together, and know that it was the journey itself that has brought us to a place of deep intimacy with the one we love. In the final analysis, couple intimacy is about death: we have dedicated our entire life, our entire heart 'all in' with our beloved, and one of us will someday die and leave the other. Our own or our partner's death will be the final act of intimacy in this life that we will share together, and it will be, of course, very hard to tolerate. But if we have done our work well in intimacy, we will be prepared, though painful, for this final, intense intimate act. And we can be assured that love is love, and it never fades away. Once we achieve deep intimacy with our partner, not even death will break such a bond, *for you are <u>in</u> your beloved and your beloved is <u>in</u> you, and you have become <u>one</u>*.

Individual Questions to Answer and Then Share:
1. Have you felt a sense of time passing, and wanting to get it right?
2. Can you recognize areas where you have wasted time and energy?
3. Do you feel yourself 'all in' with your partner?
4. Have you contemplated the death of either of you?

Intimacy Maintenance: If you have children, set aside time for the two of you to talk about making your wills and funeral arrangements.

Intimacy Enrichment: On a planned time away together, talk about how you want to spend your 'golden years' together.

Individual Activity: Make a list of all the things than your partner means to you. This can include attributes like "you make me laugh" or events in your life together ("when you held me when my mom died"), or other characteristics ("you have been my best friend").

Couple Activity: Read your lists to each other.

Chapter 6: Intimacy in the Long Run

6.1 Married Dating

Married dates should look *way different* from going out dates. While there is nothing wrong with going out with friends for a dinner date, or to a sporting event, or even shopping, this does not qualify for an intimate married date. If you are going to spend money, spend it on a good baby sitter if you need one, or on a five star luxury hotel room. For the more budget minded, get a family member to watch the kids for a few hours, pack a picnic, and head for the State park. Take a walk together. Hold hands. Engage in a few of the six intimacies. Plan your time together to be valuable to both of you. Yes, *plan* to be intimate.

On married dates, avoid talking about kids, in-laws, money, bills, work, and if you have any, ex's.

6.2 Structuring Shared Intimacy: Weekly In-House Dates

Lots of couples say that they get their together time when the kids go to bed, but when examined, what they really mean is that they sit and watch television or play on social media, quite ignoring each other. Or they mean that they have sex once a week (and not very good sex, at that).

Setting aside a weekly in-house date is a bit more…work. It is more sophisticated than an episode of *America's Got Talent* and a quick roll in the hay before rolling over to sleep.

The weekly date should have some basic rules, and form there, creativity is the byword. It should be at least an hour long (two is better). No electronics, turn phones off. The focus is on each other. The plan is to engage in one or more of the intimacies. If the evening leads to some sexual affection, great, but that isn't the ultimate goal. Rather, you are working to establish a routine manner of working on couple intimacy. One good tool to use might be this workbook! So, what to do? A mentioned earlier, it is just as important to know what not to do or not to talk about, but if you need ideas, see the ones at the end of the workbook for each of the six intimacies.

Schedule at weekly date night, right now!

6.3 Structuring Shared Intimacy: Monthly Out of House Dates

Monthly dates out of the house should be scheduled months in advance. You can take turns in planning and surprising your beloved with what you have worked out. They should last at least a few hours, if not a whole day. Remember that the point of the date is to spend time together, not do holiday shopping, or visit with friends or relatives. Those things are nice and good, but not a real date. Also remember to avoid the topics that were outlined earlier; the goal here is to spend time in some of the six intimacies. This is not about spending loads of money, but about the intimacies you engage in. Activities that you both enjoyed together (alone, as a couple, not with friends) prior to children are a good place for ideas, as is the listing at the end of the workbook.

6.4 Structuring Shared Intimacy: Yearly Retreat

Once a year (at least) schedule at least a two night (three is better) time away together from the children, extended family, and work. Find a place that is remote, does not have electronic amusements or other strong attractions nearby. A good example is a cabin in the woods out of cell tower range.

The point of this time away is not to sightsee, socialize with others, or otherwise vacation, but to spend an extended time engaging in the six intimacies and realigning your life together.

Many will be tempted to say, 'We just don't have the time to do that.' Baloney. Plan the time in advance. You find the time to get your car serviced, so you can find the time for this. Many will be tempted to say, "We don't have the money to rent a cabin.' Baloney. Save your pocket change over the course of a year, or use the event as a Christmas gift to each other. The cabin does not have to be fancy (look into your State park system, usually very reasonable).

6.5 Structuring Shared Intimacy: Yearly Retreat Structure

Try to go away for a minimum of 48 hours; 72 is better (two or three nights). Just the two of you, no kids, no relatives, no friends dropping by. Go where you will have little distraction, like a cabin in the middle of a forest, someplace that has no T.V., wi-fi, or much cell coverage. It is ok to bring a music source, but resist being tempted to use any other feature the device may have. Plan to make your own food, not go out to restaurants. You would be surprised how those things can distract you from the task at hand. If you feel the need to call home to check on the kids, do so, but only once a day. Otherwise, turn off your phone and turn it facedown.

While you can take a walk in the woods together or build a campfire to sit near, or play a couple of hands of rummy, let these kinds of things be your only distractions from the intimacy you are doing the retreat to achieve.

You are not allowed to talk about work, kids, money, bills, in-laws and if you have any, exes.

Plan to cook simply, but with special care, and healthy. Be sure to cook together, unless one of you is a gourmet and is brilliant at cooking. Make your meals leisurely and special. Bring along real china and silverware, and nice wine glasses to use instead of paper, foam, and plastic. Check in advance if you need to bring linens and cookware, etc., and if there is a stove and refrigerator. (State parks usually have pretty good cabin facilities at a reasonable price.)

Resist bringing sleeping bags. Instead, bring satin sheets and a nice comforter. Pack good quality massage oil, and some candles. Don't forget any birth control needed, and any other special toys you both enjoy.

Reserve time on your retreat together to intentionally engage in each of the six intimacies. A good idea is to allow about two hours or so for each of them. This may seem a long time, but remember that you may need the time to get comfortable enough in the environment that has no distractions to enter into the intimate space together. Go slow, be gentle with each other. It may seem artificial to set a schedule of 12 hours to cover six intimacies, but by doing this, you will sure to give each of them fair attention, and you will find that transitioning into each will be easier because they are scheduled.

In addition to the time you set for the six intimacies, plan a couple of hours to exchange responses to the following questions:

- What am I doing well at in our relationship?

- What could I be doing better in our relationship?

- What do you need more of from me?

- What has changed in our relationship over the past year?

Some of the time spent in intimacies lend themselves to pretty much any environment (it can be very spiritual to sit and watch the sunrise together, for example), while others may be best shared in mutually comfortable surroundings (lovemaking on a mattress instead of the mosquito-infested meadow). Use your common sense, and above all *communicate* clearly, gently, and non-reactively. Of course, you can certainly spend more time on each intimacy, or repeat the time on any particular intimacy you would like. Leaving space for spontaneity is very wise.

For ideas about what to actually do for each of the intimacies, see 'Intimate Acts' in the Appendix.

Appendix: Intimate Acts to Try

General Activity Ideas

- Play together: a board game, cards, a puzzle, word games, toss a ball outdoors, video game.
- Read to each other.
- Have a picnic.
- Write a love letter or poem to your beloved.

Intellectual

- Read the same book, and discuss.
- Spend an afternoon in a museum.
- Watch a documentary together.
- Learn something new together.
- Collect wildflowers together.
- Go on a bird watching outing.
- Learn some riddles and trade them with each other (no hints).
- Go to a concert together.
- Work a puzzle together.

Emotional

- Get a copy of Walt Whitman's *Leaves of Grass* or Kahlil Gibran's *The Prophet* and read passages aloud to each other.
- Find a film that evokes great emotion in you, and share it. Don't forget to discuss why.
- Sit close together and look at all of the old photos and videos from your shared past.
- Review which gifts the other has given to you that have been the most moving/precious.

- Spend some time eye gazing.
- Watch a sunrise or sunset together.
- Look through your wedding photos together.
- Share an emotional event from your childhood that you have never shared with your partner.
- Check in often: 'How are you feeling right now?'

Physical

- Brush each other's hair.
- Learn basic massage techniques and try them out.
- Offer a foot massage.
- Give each other manicures or pedicures.
- Share a long kiss.
- Give a tiny kiss to each of the other's fingertips (or toes!)
- Compete to be the first to touch when you have been away from each other.
- Talk about your own favorite way to be held, and why.
- Make a nice plate of finger foods to share, and then feed each other.
- Research home-made spa treatments and then treat your partner.
- Discover how lightly you can touch each other with just finger tips, and stroke all exposed skin.
- Make your own 'coffee' scrub and hop in the shower or bath to scrub each other.
- One of you give the other a full body massage, with both of you in the nude; no sex permitted.

Sexual

- Write out your erotic-sexual fantasy wish list, and then share it with your beloved.
- Research and learn concepts of the spiritual side of sex.
- Determine which of you initiates sex the most, them make a point of sharing initiation.
- Find out how each of you best likes to have sex initiated, then DO that.
- Learn how to give an erotic massage, then offer this to your beloved.
- Work out a simple erotic role play. Be sure you both agree to its theme and content.

- Take an 'erotic' mini-vacation: book a cabin or a good motel room for a weekend and engage in sensual pleasures: dinner out, good wine, chocolate, mutual massages, and lots of sex!

Spiritual

- Read a book on spirituality together, then discuss.

- Pray or meditate silently, together.

- Read scriptural passages aloud to each other, for example Song of Songs from the Bible.

- Listen to a piece of classical music together, and cuddle.

- Write a prayer for your partner and then read it aloud, like you did your vows.

- Pray *for* each other.

- Choose a place of worship and attend together.

- Agree to take a long walk together in nature (beach, forest) and stay silent.

- Go someplace where there is little light pollution, and lie on the ground together and look at the stars.

- Find scents you both enjoy that make you feel 'spiritual' (candles or incense).

- Find a saying or piece of scripture that you use as a kind of ritual for when you are apart. (Genesis 31:49) for example.

Difficult

- Complete this workbook!

- Identify a few current minor issues or areas of difficulty between you, and select one to thoroughly discuss. Remember, if you start to react, pause the conversation until you can self-calm.

- Identify one or two ongoing (life of the relationship) issues that never seem to get resolved. Instead of trying to solve the issue, discuss how you can cope with it.

- Set aside some time to share something you need more of in your relationship. To do this, follow these rules: make 'bullet point' notes on what you will be covering in your sharing. Be sure you start every bullet point with the word 'I'. Your partner is not permitted to interrupt you, but can respond at the end of your presentation.

- Work out a 'family mission statement.'

- Realign your individual, couple, and family priorities.

About the Author

Bill, with the direct and unwavering support of Anne, his wife of 37 years, is in private clinical counseling practice in Altoona, PA, The practice is called "Gentle Counseling", echoing Bill's first two books with Loving-Healing Press, and his work with abused children, teens, and adults. Between them, Bill and Anne have over sixty years of experience in human services, ministry, and clinical care of hurting people. Their new wire-haired terrier, Abbi, with Anne's handling, is working at becoming a therapy dog for the practice. In their spare time, Bill, Anne, and Abbi spend time at their cabin on Shaffer Mountain in Bedford County, PA.

Bibliography

Gibran, K. (1921). *The prophet*. New York: A.A. Knopf.

Gottman, J. (2018). *Seven principles for making marriage work*. S.L.: Cassell Illustrated.

Morin, J. (1996). *The erotic mind*. London: Headline.

Ogden, G. (2018). *Expanding the practice of sex therapy: The neuro update edition-an integrative approach for... exploring desire and intimacy*. S.l.: Routledge.

Perel, E. (2006). *Mating in captivity: Reconciling the erotic + the domestic*. New York: HarperCollins.

Ratner, H. (2012). *Solution focused brief therapy: 100 key points and techniques*. London: Routledge.

Schnarch, D. (2009). *Passionate marriage: Love, sex and intimacy in emotionally committed relationships*. New York: W.W. Norton & Co.

Schnarch, D. (1991). *Constructing the sexual crucible: An integration of sexual and marital therapy*. New York: Norton.

Whitman, W. (1897). *Leaves of grass*. London: G.P. Putnam's Sons.

Wincze, J. P., & Carey, M. P. (2009). *Sexual dysfunction: A guide for assessment and treatment*. Enskede: TPB

Index